THE
PROJECT OFFICE

*A Key to Managing
Projects Effectively*

THE
PROJECT OFFICE

*A Key to Managing
Projects Effectively*

THOMAS R. BLOCK
J. DAVIDSON FRAME

CRISP.
Learning
Menlo Park, California

Editor-in-Chief: *William F. Christopher*

Project Editor: *Kay Keppler*

Editor: *Regina Preciado*

Cover Design: *Kathleen Barcos*

Cover Production: *Russell Leong Design*

Book Design & Production: *London Road Design*

Printer: *Phoenix Color Corp.*

Library of Congress Card Catalog Number 97-68245

ISBN 1-56052-443-X

02   10 9 8 7

CONTENTS

LIST OF ACRONYMS

CCB	Change Control Board
CMM	Capability Maturity Model
CPM	Critical Path Method
FDA	Food and Drug Administration
PERT	Program Evaluation and Review Technique
PMBOK	Project Management Body of Knowlegde
PMI	Project Management Institute
PMP	Project Management Professional
RFP	Request for Proposal
SEI	Software Engineering Institute
WBS	Work Breakdown Structure

To Barbara Block

and

Katherine Frame

INTRODUCTION

Project management has been called the accidental profession. Typically, we become project managers by accident. Perhaps we are named project manager as a reward for good technical performance. Once we receive the project manager designation, we continue in this accidental mode by learning our jobs through trial and error.

Companies can no longer afford to manage by accident. We live and work in a time of rapid change, new challenges, new opportunities. To manage the challenges and exploit the opportunities, successful companies continuously change themselves—they create new products, develop new services, design new processes, adopt new strategies and supporting programs, establish new organizational structures. How do companies make such changes? By organizing and managing successful projects. Projects are the vehicle of change. Projects create the company's future.

As project-focused, team-based activities increasingly dominate how we conduct our affairs at work, it becomes obvious that we need to approach project management in a more conscious fashion. As individuals, we need to learn the tools of the trade in the areas of scheduling, budgeting, allocating resources, defining needs, managing requirements, and so on. At the level of the organization, we need to know how to support the efforts of those who carry out the company's projects.

This book is written for managers who are trying to discover how best to implement projects in their organizations. It focuses on nurturing project management capabilities by establishing and maintaining a project office. It does this by reviewing the functions that project offices can carry out and showing how project offices can be set up to support these functions.

Fortune magazine has identified project management as a career path of choice. Tom Peters, in his book *Liberation Management,* suggests that project management is a key to organizational survival and success into the next millennium. Clearly, project management offers a significant approach to operating successfully in today's chaotic times. Project offices help organizations ensure that, as they struggle to survive and thrive in the turbulence, they can get it right!

I.

EVOLUTION OF
THE PROJECT OFFICE

P ROJECT MANAGEMENT BECAME A major approach to managing business and government undertakings in the 1990s. Although men and women have been carrying out projects for thousands of years, it is only today that project management has become a recognized management discipline.

Phenomenal Growth

The explosive growth of project management can be seen in several ways. For example, the Project Management Institute (PMI) had a membership that ranged from 6,000 to 8,000 for many years. Then in the mid-1990s, membership suddenly grew to more than 25,000. Similarly, in the 1980s, 50–60 people were certified annually as Project Management Professionals. By the mid-1990s, this figure climbed to 3,000 a year.

The newfound importance of project management was not lost on the management community. In his book

Liberation Management (1983), Tom Peters identified mastery of project management as a key to survival and success in chaotic times. In 1995, two articles in *Fortune* identified project management as the career path of choice.

What is Project Management?

Project management is a management approach concerned with getting the job done—on time, within budget, and according to specifications. The primary focus is on results. When professionals carry out projects, they direct their efforts to achieve clearly defined results—say, building a bridge, developing a new database system, designing a training curriculum, writing advertising copy, or cleaning the garage.

Infinite resources are not available to apply to projects. Project managers operate under the universal triple constraints of time, budget, and specifications. Time constraints can be brutal. To be competitive, organizations must do their jobs faster, faster, faster. It is not unusual for a project team to be asked to achieve a nine-month job in seven months. Budget constraints demand that project teams do more with less. Constraints on specifications limit the range of discretionary action that project teams can employ in producing deliverables.

A collection of management tools has emerged to help project teams do their jobs. Schedules help teams handle time constraints. Project management makes heavy use of specific scheduling tools such as PERT/CPM networks, Gantt charts, and milestone charts. Managing budget constraints is made possible by means of another set of tools, such as S-curves, earned value analysis, and assorted cost estimating methodologies. Finally, the specification constraint is handled by needs/requirements definition techniques and well-established change management procedures, such as configuration management.

One of the most distinguishing features of project management is that work is usually carried out by cross-functional teams of borrowed resources. For example, on a software development project, software designers are borrowed from the design shop. When they have finished their work, they return to the design shop. Similarly, testing is carried out by borrowed resources coming from the testing shop, code writing by borrowed resources from the programming shop, and so on. This approach is called matrix management.

Work carried out under the project management approach radically differs from work executed in traditional functional organizations. In traditional organizations, professionals do their jobs in an environment in which job roles are readily defined and management control is rooted in chains of command.

A Solution to Modern Business Challenges

The project management approach is well suited to today's chaotic business environment, where nothing seems to be clear. This environment is characterized by such phenomena as downsizing, outsourcing, inverted pyramids, reengineering, customer focus, worker empowerment, and the need for cross-functional solutions to complex problems.

Project management's ascendance is closely tied to the new business environment. Consider, for example, some of the advantages of matrix management in today's chaotic world. Using borrowed resources enables organizations to use resources cost effectively. You borrow whom you need, employ their skills, and then send them back to their functional home when they are done. Matrix management also enables organizations to put together cross-functional teams reflecting the multifunctional substantive needs associated with today's business solutions. A team can be assembled by recruiting someone from the sales department, someone from engineering, someone from finance, and so on. Finally, when implemented properly, matrix management enables employees to acquire broad experience of their organization's activities.

Before the 1940s, projects were implemented haphazardly. During World War II, the exigencies of the war forced governments to seek more systematic ways of carrying out projects. Project management emerged as a discipline in the 1950s, primarily in the construction and defense sectors of the economy. Today virtually all industries employ project management. Its most explosive growth is occurring in knowledge-based industries such as information technology, telecommunications, finance, and pharmaceuticals.

The Project Office

As the practice of project management has grown, so has the demand for a systematic method of implementation. Organizations have acted quickly to acquire project scheduling software, send employees to project management training programs, and even establish project management academic degree programs. Companies can do something else to enhance their project management: establish project offices.

Defining a Project Office

The project office is staffed by project management professionals who serve their organization's project management needs. The duties and functions of project offices vary by organization, although in recent years differing roles have converged (see Figure 1). Project offices today carry out some or all of the following functions:

- *Supply project management support to the project team.* Project office personnel can make the lives of project team members easier by assuming administrative chores for project scheduling, report production and

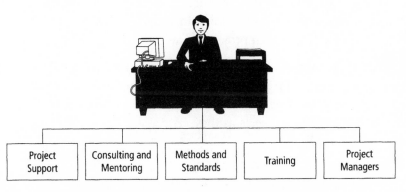

Figure 1. Project office—a full-service provider

distribution, project management software operation, and maintenance of the "visibility room" and the project workbook.

- *Providing the organization with project management consulting and mentoring.* As organizations move toward "projectizing" their efforts, they need to develop personnel who can serve as internal project management consultants, thereby providing the organization with the expert insights it needs to execute projects effectively. These consultants usually are housed within project offices.

- *Developing and maintaining project management methodologies and standards for the organization.* For organizations to carry out projects consistently, common methodologies and standards must be developed and promulgated. Project offices are well suited to do this.

- *Providing project management training to the organization.* Adopting project management approaches requires organizations to train employees in project management principles. Training material and instructors can originate in project offices.

- *Providing the organization with managers who can run projects.* Project offices can house professional project managers who can be assigned to carry out the organization's projects as they arise.

Each of these functions of the project office is treated in separate chapters later in this book.

The Need for a Project Office

If an organization carries out projects only occasionally, there is no need to develop systematic capabilities to engage in project efforts. In this case, establishing a project office would be analogous to killing mosquitoes with a shotgun. However, as an organization directs more of its energy toward implementing projects, an *ad hoc* approach to project management leads to inefficiencies and can even be dangerous. With more projects, the need for a project office becomes more compelling.

When a project office is established, the organization can develop a consistent approach to implementing projects. Beyond this, if the project office is configured to serve the whole organization, it can play an important role in integrating organization-spanning, cross-functional activities. It can also nurture project management professionalism. Employees engaged in project work are more likely to achieve and maintain the highest level of insights on and attitudes toward project management (see Figure 2).

Today's project offices have antecedents in the project offices of the defense and construction industries, which have always been project-focused and organized to centralize project management activities in a single place. However, these traditional project offices were different from those we see emerging today. They generally served the needs of a single, large, complex project. For example, if a project to build a fighter aircraft was initiated, a project office (often called a program office) would be established. In the civilian sector, a project to build a coal-fired power

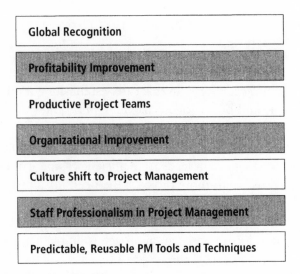

Figure 2. Progressive benefits of a project office

plant would be run through a project office established specifically to serve the project's needs.

In contrast to this traditional approach, today's emerging project offices serve the broader project management needs of the organization. They are not set up to handle a specific project, but rather to serve multiple projects and the organization overall.

II.

PROJECT
ADMINISTRATIVE SUPPORT

O NE OF THE REALITIES OF project management is that as projects get larger, the administrative chores associated with them grow explosively. On very large projects (for example, major defense acquisitions) more than half of the life-cycle cost of the project is dedicated to maintaining administrative infrastructure. Large projects have proportionately greater administrative requirements than small projects, simply because there is so much more to track.

Even on small projects, administrative chores can be substantial. With a two-person team, only one channel needs to be maintained to enable the team members to communicate. With a three-person team, three channels need to be maintained; with a four-person team, six channels; and with a five-person team, ten channels (see Figure 3). These communication channels reflect information that must be managed. Memos must be written and filed, more meetings must be held, and decisions must be documented and archived. In general, the following formula describes the relationship between the number of team members and the number of possible channels that need to be maintained:

Number of channels $= n(n-1)/2$, or $(n^2 - n)/2$

where *n* equals the number of members on the team. This formula shows that communication requirements

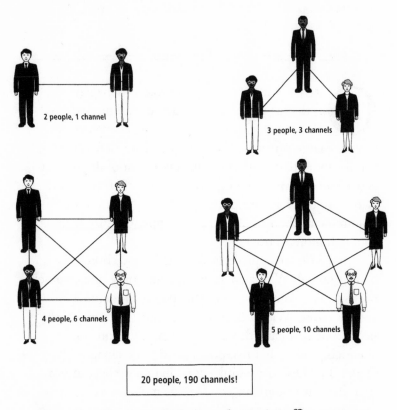

2 people, 1 channel

3 people, 3 channels

4 people, 6 channels

5 people, 10 channels

20 people, 190 channels!

Figure 3. **Growing complexity makes project offices necessary**

grow exponentially as teams get larger. A small team of 20 people requires 190 communication channels!

Thus, project team members can spend enormous amounts of time taking care of administrative chores, which detracts from working on the project issues of team-building, working with customers, and solving the problems that arise as the project is implemented. Team members should make use of administrative support to help them take care of these administrative chores, freeing time to resolve project issues.

Project Office Chores

Through project offices, team members can get the administrative support they need. Following is a list of some of the support that project office staff can offer the team.

Schedule Maintenance

Project scheduling provides the team with information on who should be doing what and when the work will be accomplished. This information is often maintained on computerized scheduling systems that run on personal computers, such as *ABT Project Workbench, Microsoft Project,* or *Project Scheduler.* When user-friendly scheduling software first emerged in the early 1980s, it was generally expected that project team members would learn how to use it and would employ it on their projects. However, it quickly became obvious that having team members sitting at computers throughout the life of the project was not a good use of their time and skills.

One of the early functions of project offices was to supply people who could maintain project schedules on behalf of project team members. These people should be skilled in using scheduling software. They work continually with team members, updating the schedule when appropriate.

Time Sheet Maintenance

Filling out time sheets is one of the curses of life for project team members. Periodically (usually weekly) they must fill out a form that shows how they have allocated their time in project work. If employees work on more than one task (a common phenomenon among project workers), they must report how they spent their time across a broad range of activities, whose names and code numbers they may not recall.

The project office staff can help maintain time sheets. They can meet frequently with project team members (perhaps once or twice a month) to discover what task commitments they have made. With this information, they can put together time sheet reports that itemize the tasks that have been undertaken during the reporting period. Project team members need merely supply the number of hours they spent on individual tasks.

Report Production and Distribution

As projects are carried out, they generate results which must be written up and distributed to those who need to know. Some of these reports are directed to customers, who want to learn what progress has been achieved. Others are more routine presentations of project status that must be made periodically (say, once a month). Project office staff can create and distribute such reports.

Visibility Room Maintenance

On bigger projects (those that last more than three or four months), it is a good idea to establish visibility rooms. The physical traits of the visibility room can vary considerably, ranging from "virtual" space on a computerized bulletin board to a small office to a sophisticated facility crammed with all manner of electronic gear. Administrative staff can maintain visibility rooms (for example, keeping a library of pertinent project management literature, maintaining the project history).

Archiving

As projects are completed, they generate large quantities of data which may be lost if no attempt is made to archive it systematically. It is important to make decisions based on experience rather than gut feeling. Consequently, someone should collect and archive data on how projects are implemented. If such information is maintained for many projects, the organization will develop a meaningful database that reflects its project experiences. The information contained in this database can guide future decisions.

Reports Consolidation and Distribution

Project teams often generate many reports on such things as monthly project progress, testing procedures and results, and research findings. Although team members still have to produce these reports through their own efforts, the project office can help by performing the library functions of report consolidation, storage, and distribution.

Project Workbook Maintenance

Project workbooks keep track of what actions have been carried out on the project. For example, if the design of the deliverable has been modified, this change will be reported in the workbook. If project procedures have been altered, the workbook will be updated to reflect this fact. By maintaining the project workbook, the project office can take a major administrative burden off the shoulders of the project team.

Software Operation

Projects make heavy use of computers, which are valuable in aiding the project team to develop schedules, budgets, and resource allocations. A wide array of project management software has been developed to help team members keep track of what they are doing. High-end software packages help project teams on complex projects (for example, building a nuclear power plant or implementing a corporate-wide management information system). Programs such as *Project, Project Scheduler,* or *ABT Project Workbench* work well on smaller projects.

Staffing

The administrative support function usually does not require highly experienced and skilled project professionals, but does require solid administrative capabilities. For example, administrative personnel should be familiar with basic office procedures, such as filing correspondence and preparing and reproducing reports. The support staff should also be computer literate, understanding basic word processing and spreadsheet programs.

Specialized knowledge can be gained through on-the-job and classroom training. For example, support personnel can receive training on the particular scheduling software product that is chosen to maintain project cost and schedule data. Experienced project management consultants working in the project office can be used from time to time to ensure that the administrative support efforts are on target.

III.

PROJECT MANAGEMENT CONSULTING AND MENTORING

A S ORGANIZATIONS BECOME MORE sophisticated in carrying out projects, their need for expert knowledge on the intricacies of project management grows. When organizations begin to implement project management, they typically do so in an *ad hoc* fashion. For example, the basic scheduling tool they are likely to use is a milestone chart, which simply ties key events to dates. As more projects are completed, management may recognize that the activities of one project affect progress on others. They may ask that projects be scheduled using computerized scheduling software that links project components and tracks projects across the organization. Scheduling no longer can be *ad hoc*. The people who maintain computerized schedules must possess specialized scheduling skills.

The need for specialized knowledge applies to a wide array of activities, including scheduling, budgeting, writing proposals, assessing vendors, selecting projects, managing risk, identifying needs and requirements, managing change to requirements, coping with project politics, and building authority. The organization may need access to project management consultants with extensive project management knowledge and experience. Top management can use the consultants' guidance to develop strategic insights into the direction the organization should take, while project workers can pick the consultants' brains to resolve day-to-day project issues.

If project management consulting is required only occasionally, a cost-effective way to obtain consulting insights is through consulting firms and universities. However, if an organization has made a major commitment to conducting its affairs by means of projects, it will require constant access to project management expertise. Using internal consultants is a good way to keep this expertise readily available. Internal project management consultants usually are housed in a project office.

In the 1990s, a new term emerged to describe a substantial portion of what internal consultants do: mentoring. The mentoring concept emphasizes that the consultants' primary job is *not* to solve the organization's problems. Rather, it is to provide employees of the organization with the insights and knowledge they need to solve the challenges of project management by themselves.

The Role of Mentors and Consultants

The role of internal project management consultants and mentors evolves continuously. Today it focuses on several fairly well defined activities, including:

- Offering proposal support

- Providing project start-up assistance

- Offering just-in-time responsiveness to the organization's project needs

- Conducting risk assessments

- Providing assistance for project recovery

- Mentoring of senior management

Each of these activities will be discussed in turn.

Proposal Support

Capable project management consultants have had years of project experience. They have been involved in the writing and evaluation of many proposals and can bring valuable insights to the organization about developing project proposals. They can assist in proposal development in three ways:

- They can introduce effective project management procedures to the organization. They can show their colleagues how developing a proposal is a project in its own right and how a well-managed proposal development effort requires good management practices. They can also introduce techniques used by many companies to write winning proposals, such as employment of pink team and red team reviews of the emerging proposal.

- They can write the portion of the proposal that covers the project management methodologies that will be employed to carry out the proposed work. Many requests for proposal (RFPs) ask that proposers describe the project management approach they will use to conduct their work.

- They can review proposals. Taking the viewpoint of an outsider, they can critique proposals, highlighting their strengths and weaknesses.

Project Start-up Assistance

Project success is often tied to how well a project is launched. If it gets off on the wrong foot, failure may be built into the project from day one. Project management consultants can introduce their colleagues to good project start-up practices. For example, they can teach team members how to develop first-rate project charters and scope statements. They can also design and facilitate project kickoff meetings. Once team members get practice in holding two or three kickoff meetings, they won't need the project consultants' guidance in the future.

Just-in-Time Response to Project Needs

As projects are carried out, many unexpected events occur. An important vendor might go bankrupt, a contract dispute might develop, or the customer might release new funds to get the project completed sooner. Expected challenges arise as well. New project staff need guidance on how to schedule project efforts, budget cutbacks that require the project team to do more with less, and new project management procedures introduced into the organization. An important function of project consultants and mentors is simply to be there–to be available to provide staff with whatever project management assistance they need.

If the project consultants are to provide just-in-time response to handle project needs, they must be knowledgeable and experienced in a broad range of project efforts. If they do not possess personal knowledge of a solution to a problem, they should be able to identify sources of information to enable them and the team to resolve issues.

Risk Assessments

Many projects fail because promises are made at the outset that cannot be kept. An account executive might promise an important customer that a six-month job can be achieved in four months. If it truly is a six-month job, then failure has been programmed into the project. The project team will not be able to deliver the product or service within the promised time frame. As the schedule slips, the project probably also will face cost overruns. Meanwhile, the customer loses confidence in the project team because they cannot keep the account executive's promises.

Organizations are turning to risk analysis before contracts are signed to assess the promises they make to customers. Project management consultants review promised delivery dates and budget estimates to determine whether they are realistic. When the consultants have completed their assessments, they write up their findings in a report.

The consultants do not have the power to kill bad projects, but their findings will alert management to problems before commitments are made and contracts are signed.

Consultants can carry out risk assessments at other times, as well. They can be brought in any time circumstances suggest that project risks should be reviewed.

Project Recovery

Recent research in the information technology arena suggests that only a small portion of project teams get the job done on time, within budget, and according to specifications. Most fail to perform adequately on at least one of the triple constraints. Consequently, many projects exist in a *recovery* condition—that is, special efforts must be made to get them back on track.

Getting a project on track demands a high level of experience and sophistication. For example, when projects slip their schedules, it is tempting to throw resources at them to catch up. Yet this solution may exacerbate rather than solve the problem. Experienced project management consultants have the skills to approach project recovery in a reasonable fashion. They know what works and what does not. They will employ scheduling tools (such as PERT/CPM charts) to identify the best way to configure tasks to accelerate performance. They have the business knowledge to assess the business implications of different courses of action.

Mentoring of Senior Management

Implementing a project management approach in organizations often entails undertaking substantial changes in the ways companies do business. Functional-driven hierarchies must give way to flattened, cross-functional structures. For the project management approach to work, it must receive the full support of senior management.

A common problem encountered by many organizations is top management's ignorance of what project management is. Project management consultants and mentors coming from the project office can educate managers about project management and the requirements that this management approach places on the organization. For example, effective cost control on projects demands that organizations adopt an activity-based accounting system. This system may be an alien concept to managers nurtured on general ledger accounting systems. Project management mentors can educate managers on the role of activity-based accounting. Without such mentoring, they may resist attempts to abandon tried-and-true general ledger accounting.

Traits of Project Consultants and Mentors

Management that plans to staff a project office with project management consultants and mentors should plan to consider two levels of consultants. *Standard consultants* have at least five years of project management experience and are skilled in basic scheduling, budgeting, and resource allocation practices; *senior consultants* possess these same skills, but beyond this have 10 to 15 years of hands-on experience running significant projects.

For project management consultants and mentors to operate effectively, the people with whom they work must perceive them to be superlatively qualified to do their jobs. They must be credible. Their knowledge and competence is their primary source of authority. If people in the organization do not see them to be the ultimate experts in project management, then they offer their organizations little value.

One way to establish their expert authority is to hire only people who have been certified as project management professionals. Achievement of certification means that these people have demonstrated a high level of mastery of the knowledge-based skills of project management. Beyond this, the consultants and mentors must have fought in the trenches of project management. They must be able to demonstrate that they are battle-scarred practitioners and not ivory-tower theoreticians.

While the consultants and mentors should be experts in the standard areas of scheduling, budgeting, and resource allocation, they must also be strong management generalists with a solid grasp of marketing, finance, contracting, and human relations principles. Much of consultants' value lies in their ability to integrate project issues into the broader business context. As management generalists, they are positioned to do this.

A problem that some organizations will have in developing a strong group of consultants and mentors is that these people do not come cheap. The salaries of senior consultants and mentors fall in the range of salaries offered to the most senior engineers in technical organizations. However, well-chosen consultants and mentors should be able to pay their own way. To understand this, consider the following story.

> Tom, who directed the project office at a major systems integration firm, received a desperate phone call from an account manager in charge of a major bank software implementation. The project had been planned hastily before bid and now more hours of effort were needed than originally thought. The project was in a sorry state, and the account manager could not answer the bank's inquiries about a completion date. The bank was threatening to terminate the contract.

> After listening to the account manager's story, Tom told her that he could supply a consultant who would be billed at $15,000 per month. The account manager responded: "That's fine. The consultant's wages are insignificant compared to what we could lose if we don't get this project on track."

> The consultant worked out the project problems in three months at a cost of $45,000 to the project. It was estimated that if the project had failed, it would have cost the company a loss of $7.2 million.

IV.

DEVELOPING
PROJECT MANAGEMENT
STANDARDS AND METHODS

P ROJECT OFFICES, AS THE guardians of project management expertise within the organization, carry out, among others, this important function: they maintain project management standards and methods. If the project management approach is to be implemented well, it is vital that everyone within the organization march to the beat of a single drummer. That beat is embedded in the project management standards and methods established by the project office.

With well-established standards and methods, project staff have guidance on the steps they should take to produce deliverables that are consistent from project to project. A fundamental precept of the Software Engineering Institute's capability maturity model is that effective organizations have established methods and procedures that lead to processes that can be replicated. In project management, we attempt to follow SEI's leadership by establishing methods and procedures that lead to replicable outcomes on our projects. Standards and methods should be developed and maintained in several areas, including implementing project management procedures, maintaining documentation, and identifying appropriate software.

Standards for Implementing Procedures

As projects move away from an *ad hoc* structure toward being an important part of an organization's operations, the project office must create consistent project management procedures to apply across departments and divisions. This task takes time and isn't easy, but without consistent procedures, project management efforts are likely to degenerate into chaos. Instead of helping the organization to operate more efficiently, the introduction of project management with poor procedures can hurt the organization.

Developing consistent project management procedures entails a delicate balancing act. Procedures must be detailed enough to provide meaningful guidance on how projects should be carried out, but they should not be so detailed that they become an oppressive bureaucratic burden that squelches innovation and initiative. One of the first steps people working in a project office should take if they are to develop and implement project management procedures is to determine how encompassing and detailed the procedures should be.

Project management procedures cannot be created in a vacuum. Those who develop the procedures must maintain constant communication with the professionals who will implement them. Some of these people work directly on project teams. Others may be affiliated with functional groups such as the purchasing department, maintenance department, and design shop. Still others might be categorized as traditional customers, people who will use the outputs of the project effort. If effective procedures are to be developed and implemented, all the key stakeholders must accept them and be willing to work with them. The best way to get their support is to let them play an active role in reviewing the emerging procedures.

The areas of project activity that can be handled through procedures are limitless. Following are some of the more significant project activities that should be defined by procedures.

Bid-Preparation Procedures

In organizations that bid on project work, the entire range of bid-preparation activity should be covered by well-defined procedures. For example, clearly define the steps needed for assigning a proposal manager, selecting the proposal writing team, establishing a proposal development schedule, liaising with the print shop, and getting management approvals.

Project Selection Procedures

Project success or failure often hinges on picking winners and avoiding losers. Systematic project selection procedures must be established to identify potential winners. The project office can choose from a broad array of project selection methodologies, ranging from benefit-cost ratios and peer review to the Murder Board. Implement an objective process that enables the organization to choose projects based on their merits, not emotional or political factors.

Work Breakdown Structure Construction

The work breakdown structure (WBS) used in implementing projects shows how the pieces of the project fit together and provides the basis for developing bottom-up estimates of project costs. WBSs can be constructed in several ways, and the project office must supply explicit instructions on what approach to take. For example, should the WBS be product-oriented or task-oriented? How many levels deep should the WBS be?

Change Management Procedures

Project requirements invariably change. The project office should prescribe a clearly defined change management process. For example, the office may promote a configuration management approach to managing change, which would define how change requests would be initiated, to whom they should be directed, the role of a change control board (CCB), and so on.

PERT/CPM Network Procedures

An important project management scheduling tool is the PERT/CPM network, which identifies the project's critical path and shows how tasks are interrelated. Because

PERT/CPM networks can be configured in so many ways, the project office should establish a standard approach. One way the project office can do this is to create template PERT/CPM charts that project workers can use in scheduling. The template approach is especially effective in managing structured efforts, such as installing switches in a telecommunications project, going through FDA approval processes, or laying housing foundations in a large real estate development.

Risk Assessment Procedures

Project risks can be identified and mitigated when organizations employ systematic risk assessment procedures. The project office should develop and maintain a checklist of the bad things that can happen on projects and prescribe ways of assessing their effects. Many approaches exist to facilitate risk impact analysis, from scenario-building to Monte Carlo simulations. The project office should also suggest ways of handling risks, focusing on such established approaches as risk avoidance and risk transfer.

Documentation Standards

Projects are generally document-intensive. The origins of a project are often rooted in paper, such as when a proposal development team responds to a request for proposal. The proposal itself is a document. Budget and resource requests, scope statements, monthly progress reports, change orders, and other requirements are a small sample of the documents generated in association with a project.

A project office often provides guidance on what documents to use, when to use them, and how to process them. By fulfilling this role, the project office enhances communication within the organization, ensuring that project participants do their jobs consistently. As always, the project office staff must balance the desire for consistent processes against the need for reasonable flexibility. A key task is to identify what documents should be standardized. Following is a sampling of some documents that should be standardized by the project office.

Status Reports

Status reports are issued regularly (often once a week) to update team members on project progress. Typically, they contain data on cost and schedule performance for the reporting period. These project actuals are contrasted against the plan, enabling the team members to identify cost and schedule variances. They are important tools for project control. The project office should assume lead responsibility for designing status reports that can be used across the organization; the project office should determine what kinds of information the status reports contain and how this information is presented.

Time Sheets

Most project-focused organizations have their employees fill out time sheets (usually weekly), on which employees identify how they allocated their time across projects during the reporting period. Theoretically, an analysis of these time sheets should reveal how employees spend their time. Regrettably, time sheets generate highly imperfect information. While some of the deficiencies of time sheet reporting are tied to dishonest reporting (for example, the worker who inflates time reports to look busy), many errors occur because workers have not been given consistent policies for reporting their time allocations. Items that need to be clarified include such things as how overtime and overhead work should be reported and how workers should split time allocations when they work on multiple projects.

Change Order

One thing the project team can count on is that requirements will change, so it is important that the forms associated with change orders be developed carefully by the project office. Change request forms are needed to trigger the change management process. When change requests are approved, change implementation forms are directed to the individuals and groups who must implement the change. Change request disposition forms provide information on the decision to approve or reject a change request.

Software Standards

Project offices play a central role in establishing standards for software that will be used to manage projects. As organizations adopt project-focused operations, one of the first management issues they attempt to clarify is to identify a software scheduling package that should be used for all projects. Beyond this, they help select a single standard for word processors and spreadsheets. This attention to software standards is important for several reasons. First, the use of a single standard enhances communication within the organization. Workers in one department can understand software-generated reports that originate in another department. If necessary, employees can even swap data diskettes to transfer project-related data to each other.

Second, adopting a single software standard makes for more efficient training. The training department or the project office itself can offer regular courses on software usage for the standardized software packages. Without standards, it is difficult to offer training.

Third, by adopting standard scheduling software, organizations can maintain a database of project activities. For example, they can review how long it has taken to conduct certain kinds of tests on a dozen projects. With this information, they can improve their estimates for testing procedures on future projects.

It is unlikely that the project office will develop standards for word processing and spreadsheet software, since these standards usually are determined for the organization overall. However, the project office probably will dedicate a substantial effort to selecting a standard scheduling package. Experience shows that it is not easy to decide on such a standard. First, a recent survey shows that hundreds of scheduling packages are available, so it is difficult to sort through the bewildering array of products. Moreover, several questions must be resolved beforehand, including:

- Who will use the software? Professional schedulers? Team members? Both?

- How important is user-friendliness? Most scheduling packages offer a trade-off between user-friendliness and functionality.

- Will the software be used primarily by project teams operating independently, or will management attempt to tie project data together across all projects in the organization?

- Is it important to select a package that is favored by our customers?

- What is the "shelf price" of the software?

- What will the costs of operations and maintenance (including training) be?

A final word on establishing software standards: the project office should decide if the scheduling software it selects as the standard will lie at the heart of its planning and control efforts. If so, then this software will affect the type of documentation standards the organization will adopt, since each software package has its own approach to presenting project charts and tables.

Monitoring and Implementing Best Practices

As it guides the organization in developing standard procedures and methods for managing projects, the project office must guard against becoming self-absorbed and losing touch with best practices. Project office staff must keep up with the latest developments of project management practice. To do this, they must monitor project management and industry literature, undertake training in project-related areas (for example, courses in risk management, procurement management, and cost-benefit analysis), and attend symposia and conferences where they can learn from the project management efforts of others. By reviewing project management best practices, they can take steps to ensure that their organization's standard procedures and methods are current.

Staffing

The project office's experienced consultants should decide which standard procedures and methods should be adopted. Presumably, these men and women are aware of best practices in the industry. They understand what works and what doesn't, based on their extensive project management experience.

Implementing and maintaining standard procedures and methods usually can be carried out by less experienced people with strong administrative strengths. Even here, their efforts should be reviewed periodically by experienced project management consultants to make sure they are on target.

V.

PROVIDING PROJECT MANAGEMENT TRAINING

PROJECT OFFICES CAN PLAY an important role in offering project management training to employees in the organization. The project office can carry out this responsibility in several ways. For example, it can work closely with the training department to develop courses that would be offered through the training department. Project office staff could offer courses themselves, or they could identify and select outside vendors who would develop and deliver the course material.

Types of Training

As organizations devote more resources and energy to conducting their work on a project basis, the need for project management training grows. Project staff need this training to strengthen their ability to organize and implement their work. Workers from the functional areas (such as accounting, design, marketing, purchasing, and engineering) might also need some measure of project management training to make sure that their efforts mesh with the organization's new project focus. As organizations increase partnering arrangements with their customers, customers will need to receive the same project management training that the core project staff receive. Similarly, vendors may be required to receive some project management training.

The types of training that should be offered can vary. A study of the course offerings of several well-known project-focused companies suggests that project management related training typically falls into the following six categories.

Project Management Basics

The project management basics course is geared toward project management novices. It introduces core topics such as time, cost, and people management; the project life cycle; project management players; project politics; control; and evaluation. It usually runs two to five days. Its principal objective is to develop an understanding of what project management is, what it does, and how it fits into the organization. Owing to the short duration of the course and the limited depth of the material, students are not expected to develop strong project management skills from this training.

Advanced Project Management

Advanced project management may be a single course or a series of courses geared toward developing scheduling, cost management, and resource allocation skills. Series courses usually have titles such as "Scheduling and Cost Control" and "Project Management Applications." Unlike project management basics, students are expected to roll up their sleeves and develop project management skills through exercises, case studies, and role-playing. The number of training days associated with an advanced project management curriculum typically ranges from five to fifteen days.

Preparation for the Certification Examination

More companies and government agencies accept the Project Management Institute's Project Management Body of Knowledge (PMBOK) as the final word on project management standards. The PMBOK identifies nine broad competencies that project professionals should possess:

- Scope management

- Time management

- Cost management

- Human resource management

- Risk management

- Quality management

- Procurement management

- Communication management

- Integration management

It serves as the basis for a certification examination. Consequently, courses are offered to introduce employees to basic knowledge on the PMBOK and the certification examination. A typical PMBOK course lasts one day. Certification preparation courses generally last from one to three days.

Project Management Software Skills

It is interesting to speculate on how much of the explosive growth of interest in project management was triggered by the introduction of a project scheduling software package called *Harvard Project Manager* in the early 1980s. At a time when cumbersome personal computer software applications were selling for $1,000 each, the astonishingly attractive and user-friendly *Harvard Project Manager* was offered at a retail price of $295, but could be had at a discount for $165. This product was the first PC scheduling application to offer enormous functionality at a great price. It put project management on the map. In many organizations, developing project management capabilities was seen as synonymous to learning how to use *Harvard Project Manager.*

Today, project management software continues to have a strong impact on how organizations implement project management efforts. In many organizations, the approach to completing projects is designed around a schedule-focused software application. Consequently, the demand is great for instruction on using this software application. These courses are usually two to three days long.

Specialized Topics

Beyond studying obvious project management topics in the areas of budgeting and scheduling, project workers may benefit from investigating more specialized topics such as risk management, cost-benefit analysis, and contracting and procurement. Not every project worker need take these courses, which are aimed primarily toward those who wish to assume high levels of project management responsibility. Each of these courses can be handled as a two-day offering.

General Business Management

Project managers are like the CEOs of small enterprises. They must possess skills in a broad range of areas, from finance and marketing to customer relations. This view stands in marked contrast to the traditional perspective, where project managers were seen to be mere implementers of other people's solutions. In the traditional view, project managers were not expected to have insights outside of their narrow technical area.

To enable project managers and other project staff to develop general business management skills, they should be encouraged to take courses that cover topics such as finance, marketing, quantitative methods, information systems basics, and organizational behavior. These courses can be offered internally or by outside providers. The material can be bundled into one or two business basics courses or can be offered through separate specialized classes. The total amount of training time devoted to general business management instruction generally ranges from three to fifteen days.

Possible Training Roles of the Project Office

The need to sustain a good project management operation with training is obvious. The question that arises is: What role can the project office play in developing and delivering the training material and in coordinating the overall training effort? The real issue is whether the project office should provide the lead role, or whether it should support the training activities of the training department. The response in most organizations seems to be that the project office should do some of both. On small specialized topics (such as understanding the PMBOK and the organization's project management procedures), the project office often plays the lead role. On more traditional, substantive classroom training, it plays a support role.

Complicating matters further, what role should the project office play in working with outside vendors who supply project management training? When an organization has a strong training department, its staff generally play a lead role. When the training department is weak and the project office is strong, project office staff tend to take on the lead role.

One point is clear: whether or not the project office plays a lead role in course development, delivery, and coordination, it must assume leadership in identifying the curriculum, because the project office staff are in the best position to identify the organization's project management training needs. They understand best practices and know who many of the players are. They themselves have experienced project management training and have a good sense of what works and what does not. Following are four reasonably standard approaches to defining the training role of the project office.

Working Closely with the Training Department

In organizations with centralized training departments, it makes sense to have these departments play the lead role in developing and delivering project management courses, just as they do with other courses. Because of their centralized location, they know what the overall training program is for the entire organization and can fit the project management curriculum into the organization's broader training portfolio. This may lead to a more cohesive training effort and yield economies of operation.

In this case, the project office gives the training staff the technical information it needs to assemble a good program. For example, if the organization decides to develop its own training material, the project office staff supplies the experts who create course content. In a sense, they will be "contracted" by the training department to develop material. The training department plays the role of client, the project office the role of developer.

If management decides to use internal staff to deliver project management courses, the project office could supply the instructors, since the organization's project management expertise resides here. If the organization launches a crash training program in which many employees will receive project management training in, say, six months (a common experience), the project office may assign one of its staff to work full-time with the training department for six months.

Developing and Delivering Courses

In organizations that lack centralized training departments, it may make sense to have the project office assume a strong leadership role in developing and delivering project management courses. This is particularly true when the project office has demonstrated itself to be powerful and competent.

The project office must work closely with the training department in this effort. However, the roles have been reversed: now the project office plays the lead role while the training office plays a support role. Support from the training office might include:

- Guidance on good curriculum development practice

- Review of course material to determine its "teachability"

- Development of standard formats for producing course material

- Assistance in the production of course workbooks

- Assistance in locating rooms for instruction

- Provision of teaching technology, such as overhead projectors, LCD projectors, flip charts

Just-in-Time Training

Chapter III pointed out that in their mentoring activities, project management consultants working in the project office serve a just-in-time training function. For example, when design engineers need help in learning how to capture their activities in a work breakdown structure, they can contact an internal consultant who provides them with on-the-spot instruction on building one. When workers in the marketing department have trouble making their scheduling software perform properly, an internal consultant can offer the guidance they need.

The project office plays the lead role in supplying just-in-time training. The training department is not equipped to handle this kind of spontaneous response to the temporary training needs of the organizations' employees.

Identifying and Selecting Outside Vendors

The organization may find that it is not cost effective to develop and deliver its own project management training program, especially if courses will be offered only occasionally (say, two or three times a year). In this case, establishing project management training capabilities means identifying and selecting outside vendors who will develop and teach courses.

Identifying good outside trainers should be carried out by using standard source selection practices. First, generate a preliminary list of possible trainers, which can be done in a rather free-form fashion. Ask project specialists within and outside the organization whether they can suggest good trainers with whom they have worked.[1]

Second, contact the good prospects. In discussions with them, summarize the organization's project management training requirements. Ask about the potential contractor's training experience and capabilities. It is a good idea to develop a list of course requirements to send to prospective contractors as a follow-up to the initial discussion. Request prospective contractors to submit a short proposal describing how they can help the organization meet its project management training needs. If the training program is substantial, the project office might want to issue a formal request for proposal (RFP).

Third, after proposals have been submitted, the project office should systematically review them and select the trainers with whom it wishes to work. Organization stakeholders, including people from the functional departments as well as internal customers, should be involved in the trainer-selection effort to make sure that project office biases do not affect the selection decision.

Fourth, make an offer to the most attractive proposer. Before signing a contract, negotiate details on pricing, instructors, course content, and delivery dates.

The project office's training responsibilities do not end after an outside trainer has been contracted to implement a training program. In the post-award phase, the project office's primary task is to work with the contractor

---

1   PMI's annually published list of project management trainers and consultants is another source of information. *PM Network,* Upper Darby, Pennsylvania: Project Management Institute, Volumne II, Number 3, March, 1997.

to ensure that the program progresses smoothly. For example, the project office may play a role in advertising project management courses within the organization and generating students to attend them. The project office also has a major responsibility to monitor the quality of the contractor's training efforts and to provide the guidance needed to deliver first-rate course offerings.

Staffing

The curriculum development aspect of project management training requires the project office to supply the training effort with experienced project professionals (experts who serve as project management consultants and mentors to the organization). Based on their experience and insights, they understand what a project management training program should look like.

If the project office is asked to supply instructors for project management courses, the staffing requirements will vary according to the nature of the courses. Most courses (particularly those with a narrow technical focus) require instructors with good technical skills, but not necessarily strong project management experience. Other courses (those that attempt to convey broader management insights) should be taught by seasoned project professionals.

Working with outside trainers requires seasoned project professionals to review the capabilities of the vendors, as well as to examine course material. Once the training program is under way, administrative personnel will play a lead role.

To cope with the day-to-day administrative needs of a project management training program (whether it is managed with internal resources or uses outside contractors), the project office should be able to supply personnel who possess good administrative capabilities.

VI.

PROVIDING THE ORGANIZATION
WITH PROJECT MANAGERS

A S MORE ORGANIZATIONS CARRY OUT their activities through projects, the demand for project managers has grown. Acquiring the right person for the job is paramount. Candidates must have the proper blend of management skills and technical insights. They must also be temperamentally suited to the job–if it requires putting in 60-hour weeks, then project managers should be willing to work according to these requirements. Beyond this, project managers must be available when work needs to be conducted.

Project Office Responsibilities

One important function of the project office is to satisfy the organization's needs for project managers who can serve the organization's interest. For example, project managers can:

- Serve as internal consultants and mentors to their organizations

- Provide just-in-time training

- Help identify standards and methods that the organization should follow

In addition to performing these support functions, project managers must also be available to run projects. If the organization's business is to develop software, then project managers must be able to direct software development projects. If the company builds bridges, then project managers must be able to lead bridge construction efforts.

Personnel Management Requirements

For project offices to meet their organization's needs for a steady supply of project managers, the project office must possess human resource development capabilities. That is, it must be able to serve a personnel function. This may require the project office to:

- Identify the skill requirements for a job

- Identify individuals who can satisfy the job's requirements

- Allocate the right people at the right time

- Help the organization acquire the project managers it needs

- Assess the capabilities of project managers

Identifying the Skill Requirements

When the project office receives a request to supply a group with a qualified project manager, it must be able to identify the skills requirements for the job. These skills are both technical and managerial. For example, on a database construction project, is it necessary to have a project manager who has extensive hands-on experience in building databases? If the project is a basic implementation of a standard database package that hasn't varied in several years, can the project be led by a nontechnical person?

The project office also must be able to identify the "soft skills" needed for the job. Does the job require someone with proven leadership abilities? Should the candidate have negotiation skills? Are standard project management scheduling and budgeting skills needed?

Identifying Individuals for Particular Projects

When a request is received for a qualified project manager to run a project, the project office should be able to go through the list of possible candidates and find the one who is best suited to do the job. This means that the project office needs to develop a database that lists the qualifications of the organization's project managers.

Selecting the right person means finding someone with the right soft skills as well as technical skills. Research suggests that the best project managers possess most, if not all, of the following traits:

- Capable of understanding people needs

- Good head for details

- Strong commitment to the project and a willingness to do what it takes to get the job done

- Ability to cope with ambiguity, setbacks, and disappointments

- Awareness of the organization's goals

- Results-oriented, can-do individual

- Solid business skills, including cost-consciousness

- Good negotiating skills

- Politically savvy (knows how to influence others)

Allocating the Right People at the Right Time

The timing of resource allocations is important. Supplying the project team with Albert Einstein won't do the team much good if he comes a week too early or a week too late. To get the timing of the allocations right, the project office must be effective in several areas. For example, it must have a thorough grasp of the project's schedule. Precisely when are the project manager's services needed? Should he or she be introduced to the project early, before firm project commitments have been made? Should he or she be scheduled to stay with the project for some time after the deliverable has been handed over to customers to assure a smooth transition from the project phase to the operations phase?

The project office must be skilled in helping project managers free themselves from the multiple demands placed on their time. If good project managers are scarce, they will be inundated with requests to help out by mentoring or offering just-in-time training on many projects concurrently under way. When it is time to commit these specialists to the full-fledged management of a project, the other commitments must be pushed aside to focus on the chosen effort. If the other commitments are difficult to shed, the project manager's availability to take over a specific project may be delayed.

Acquiring the Right Project Managers

In conducting their business, managers in today's organizations are constantly engaged in make-or-buy decisions. For example, large computer manufacturers must decide whether they should produce their own computer components or buy them from outside sources.

In their attempts to acquire project managers, project offices must go through the same decision process. Questions that must be answered include: Should our organization attempt to develop project managers in-house? Should we hire experienced project managers who have gained their knowledge elsewhere? Should we simply outsource work to contracted project managers?

Each of these approaches has its strengths and weaknesses. By nurturing project managers in-house, the organization creates a group of professionals who develop project management capabilities within the context of the organization, which is good. On the other hand, these homegrown project managers will need several years before they mature into valuable and experienced project managers.

By hiring experienced project managers, the organization can acquire qualified professionals quickly. At first, their experience may not be totally relevant to the organization's specific context. Moreover, if the organization hopes to hire the best people, it should be prepared to offer very high salaries (from $110,000 to $200,000 in 1998) and to maintain these salary levels (plus associated fringe benefits) into the future.

Finally, by contracting project management activities to an outside contractor, the organization can take a flexible approach in acquiring whom it needs. However, these people may not be fully appropriate to the organization's specific context, and they certainly will be expensive. Beyond this, dependence on outsiders may lead to a hollowing of the organization's core capabilities.

Assessing Project Managers' Capabilities

If the project office becomes the "home" of project managers, then it must be able to conduct project managers' performance appraisal reviews. In a small project office, the office director performs this task. In larger offices, deputy directors who have responsibilities for pertinent functional areas will carry out the performance appraisal reviews.

The chief difficulty in assessing project managers' performance is that the evaluator, who works in the project office, does not have much opportunity to see the project manager at work on site. The performance appraisal will be based largely on feedback from the customers to whom the project manager has been assigned. While this feedback is important, it should be recognized that customers are not generally in a good position to assess the capabilities of project managers. For example, they may lack the technical skills to assess the technical merits of the project team's performance.

The Care and Feeding of Project Managers

Reengineering, downsizing, flattening, reorganizing, outsourcing, cross-functional solutions, customer focus, quick turnaround and employee empowerment all have a dramatic effect on how we manage our business efforts. Collectively they contribute to an environment that promotes the employment of project management to cope with contemporary business challenges. Today we find a strong demand for project managers who can make things happen. At the same time, we encounter a situation where the supply of good project managers is insufficient to meet demand.

If organizations want to acquire and keep highly qualified and well-motivated project managers, they must create an environment that enables them to thrive. Project offices should play a central role in this undertaking. Specifically, they should focus on four points:

- Helping project managers to upgrade their knowledge and skills

- Offering project managers guidance for their career development

- Providing project managers with the support they need to do their jobs well

- Offering attractive compensation packages

Upgrading Project Managers' Knowledge and Skills

The knowledge and skills requirements for project managers can be daunting. They may be expected to be highly skilled in the specialty area in which they work, such as database architecture, telecommunications, or bridge building. They must have skills in budgeting, scheduling, and human and material resource allocation (the traditional skills associated with project management). Beyond this, project managers should have significant insights into risk management, quality management, contract management, and a wide array of general business skills.

Some high-performing organizations offer project managers two to four weeks of training each year to hone their skills. While some of this training may be geared toward understanding their organization's products and services, most of the training focuses on developing new skills and insights, from basic project management and financial analysis to Internet literacy. Organizations that want to develop a strong group of project managers must commit significant resources to education and training.

Guidance for Career Development

Project management has achieved the status of a profession. To a large extent, this professionalism is nurtured through the auspices of the Project Management Institute (PMI), the leading society of project professionals. PMI has determined that the most effective project professionals are competent in the following areas:

- *Scope management*—the "big picture" perspective on projects, including project life cycle, implementing change management procedures, and constructing work breakdown structures (WBSs)

- *Time management*—solid scheduling capabilities with such tools as Gantt charts, milestone charts, PERT/CPM charts, and earned value

- *Cost management*—cost estimating, budgeting, economic principles, finance, rudimentary accounting, cost control, and earned value

- *Human resource management*—motivation, conflict resolution, and resource allocation

- *Risk management*—identifying risk, assessing its effects, and mitigating it

- *Quality management*—quality assurance, quality control, and engendering customer satisfaction

- *Contract management*—contracting basics, including the implications of different contract modalities and resolving disputes

- *Communication management*–"communication model"–
  sender, receiver, encoding, decoding, and feedback

- *Integration management*–tying together these eight competencies to deliver solutions on time, within budget,
  according to specifications, and with the
  highest level of customer satisfaction)

PMI administers a certification examination to assess
the extent to which individuals are competent in these
nine areas. Project offices should require project managers
to go through the certification process.*

Providing Support

Even the smartest and most energetic project managers will fail if they are not provided the support needed
to carry out a job effectively. The project office must
supply project managers with a clearly defined process
for doing their jobs. It must also supply them with necessary tools, including computer hardware and software
packages.

However, project offices do not have direct control
over many of the items that contribute to the proper support of projects. They do not control such things as order
processing systems and accounting systems. Consider the
case of accounting systems: proper cost control is difficult,
if not impossible, without an activity-based or project
accounting system, yet most organizations have general
ledger accounting systems.

---

*For more information on project management certification, contact the Project Management
Institute in the United States at (610) 734-3300, or review its web site at www.pmi.org.

One aspect of the project office's job is that of lobbying senior management to supply project staff with the equipment, training, and systems they need to do their jobs most effectively.

Attractive Compensation

The economic law of supply and demand says that if demand for an asset is high, yet supply of the asset is limited, then the price of the asset will rise. Because the demand for good project managers is high and their supply relatively low, the salaries needed to attract them are high. This is true for all levels of project managers, from entry- and mid-level to senior project managers. A survey of fifteen mulitnationals in the late 1990s found that in these companies entry-level project managers earned $45,000 to $65,000 per year; mid-level project managers, $55,000 to $85,000 per year; and senior project managers, $110,000 to more than $200,000 per year.

These salaries may appear excessive, but a solid economic rationale underlies them. Consider the following example. On a large construction project, the costs of slipping the promised delivery date will be $300,000 per month as determined by penalties and additional carrying charges. In this case, paying the very best project manager $175,000 per year to minimize the possibility of a schedule slippage is worth the expense.

VII.

VIRTUAL TEAMS AND THE PROJECT OFFICE

L ARGE ORGANIZATIONS WITH SEVERAL locations may find that project team members are geographically scattered. Project offices must learn to manage "virtual" teams as they become a greater part of the organizational workforce. At this time, however, project offices do not play a leading role in initiating virtual team efforts. Their primary role is to provide an environment that enables virtual teams to operate effectively.

It's a Virtual World

We live in a virtual world. Instead of visiting a store to buy goods, we order them through a catalog. Rather than stand in line at the bank, we do our banking electronically at an ATM machine or from a home computer. We bypass postal delivery by sending faxes and e-mails. While traveling in Latin America, we meet with our colleagues in Europe by means of videoconferencing. Technology gives us the opportunity to communicate with others (no matter where they are) instantly and cheaply. The more we use this technology, the more we recognize that geography need not constrain our activities.

The virtual project is a reality. In the late 1980s, Digital Equipment Corporation initiated steps that would enable project teams to be put together with team members coming from headquarters in New England, manufacturing in Texas, and a design shop in California. Early attempts to run virtual teams were hampered by technical limitations, but since DEC's first efforts a decade ago, these limitations have largely disappeared.

Today the focus on virtual projects has shifted from grappling with technical feasibility to resolving management issues. Some of the challenges associated with implementing virtual projects are obvious. For example, how do we handle the fact that team members may reside in different time zones?

Other challenges are more subtle. How can project offices ensure that the geographically dispersed team members have a common level of com-petence and a reasonably uniform understanding of the processes underlying a project? This issue is further complicated when team members come from different cultures where education levels and perceptions of how the world works vary.

Configuration of a Virtual Project

The project office is situated physically at the home office. It supports the efforts of the people in the field in several ways, including maintaining project management methods and standards as well as a reusable library that contains templates, algorithms, and processes that have been developed on other projects and are available for use on current efforts. Finally, the project office acts as a liaison with the organization's functional groups, such as the finance, information systems, and engineering departments. Thus, if team members in the field need support from engineering, the project office can arrange to have it provided.

Figure 4 shows a virtual project and the project office's role in supporting it. Project A is carried out remotely in geographically dispersed sites. The key project players are project team members located in Montreal, Chicago, and Singapore. An account manager who is

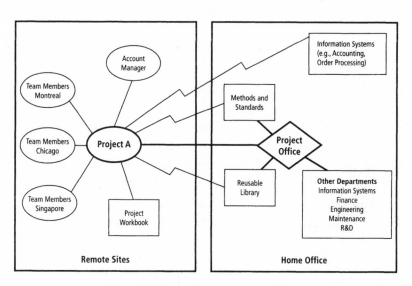

Figure 4.   A virtual project

working closely with the customer operates out of Montreal.

Communications in this configuration are largely carried out electronically, by means of telephones, e-mail, faxes, teleconferences, and videoconferences. To understand the strengths and weaknesses of virtual projects, it is necessary to grasp the key features of the technology that makes them possible.

Technology and the Virtual Project

Enormous advances in technology make the virtual office possible. With today's computer and telecommunications technology, working with someone located one thousand miles away is not much different from working with someone in the office down the hall. Following are some of the key technologies that enable virtual projects to function.

Telephone

Although the telephone was invented more than one hundred years ago, it continues to be central to business communication and serves as the backbone of the virtual project. With the telephone, two parties can carry out one-on-one oral information exchanges (old technology). Beyond this, telephone lines enable advanced communication to occur by means of teleconferences, compressed video conferences, e-mail, the Internet, and the organization's intranet (new technology).

One of the great wonders of contemporary telephone-based communications is its cheapness. Advances in technology coupled with deregulation of telecommunications has led to an astonishing drop in telephone charges. A telephone call from New York to London is billed at eight cents a minute!

Teleconferences

A cheap way for geographically dispersed project team members to get together is by teleconferencing, which allows many individuals to be part of the same telephone conversation. For this to happen, team members agree to be available for a telephone conversation at a given time. If all the team members operate in the same time zone, teleconferences can be easy to carry out with minimal inconvenience. However, if team members operate across time zones, the scheduled phone call will be more convenient for some than for others—a telephone call placed at noon in Washington, D.C., will occur at dinnertime in Europe and the middle of the night in Asia. One strategy that some companies use to minimize this problem is to change the time when calls are placed so that no one party is always inconvenienced.

Videoconferences

Videoconferencing allows you not only to hear other team members (as with teleconferencing), but to see them as well. The advantage for the team members is that when you see the people with whom you are talking, the meeting becomes more "real," even when the other attendees are sitting in a faraway studio. Beyond this, videoconferencing allows images of spreadsheets, charts, and photographs to become a part of the meeting, giving videoconferencing a strong edge over teleconferencing. A major weakness of videoconferencing is that it requires participants to have access to special telecommunications equipment. Whether the video conference is based on satellite broadcasting or compressed video, all parties need to have sending and receiving capabilities if the conference is to be truly interactive.

E-mail

The introduction of e-mail (electronic mail) into regular business transactions has revolutionized how we do business. Many people conduct most or all their written communications through e-mail; for them, using the conventional postal service has all but disappeared.

E-mail has also become a substitute for face-to-face meetings or teleconferences. One of the great attractions of e-mail is that recipients of a message do not have to be available to receive the message at the time it is sent. They need merely check their e-mail messages once or twice a day to be current on significant events. This is particularly powerful when conducting business around the world. A manager in Paris can use e-mail to request project information from an engineer in Hong Kong by sending a query just before going to bed. Upon getting up the next day, he or she can check the e-mail messages to receive the reply from Hong Kong.

E-mail capabilities have grown dramatically over time. In the early days of e-mail, all that could be transmitted were messages keyed into a computer. Today, documents, spreadsheets, graphics, video, and sound—virtually anything that can be created on a computer—can be sent by e-mail around the world for pennies.

Internet

Although the Internet has received enormous attention in the press, its value to the virtual project team is limited mostly to e-mail. The principal value of the other components of the Internet—the World Wide Web, newsgroups, etc.—is that they enable team members to access huge amounts of information quickly and cheaply. The Internet is less helpful in enabling team members to coordinate their efforts.

Intranet

In contrast to the Internet, the intranet is vital to developing and maintaining virtual project teams. It is rapidly becoming the technological platform of these teams. With intranet capabilities, geographically dispersed projects can operate as if all the team members were located at a single site. All project documents, databases, spreadsheets, schedules, and more can be made available to everyone working on the project. A team player in Kuala Lumpur can access a master schedule maintained in New Delhi and update it remotely to indicate changes in the Kuala Lumpur program.

Intranet capabilities are tied to the computer networking efforts of organizations. In the mid-1990s, Lotus Notes was the dominant platform offering organizations intranet capabilities. Toward the end of the 1990s, Microsoft NT achieved dominance.

Express Mail

Not everything in a virtual operation is intangible, or capable of being transmitted from one place to another by means of electronic signals. Some aspects of virtual projects must be physical objects. For example, a computer development project might involve building prototype circuit boards that must be shipped from the development shop to a test facility located 1,500 miles away. The emergence of courier services and express mail enables physical objects to be sent to remote sites quickly and cheaply. This capability reinforces the exponential growth of virtual activities, because it shows that geographic distances need not offer serious barriers to the transport of physical objects.

Communicating on Virtual Projects

Virtual projects present project players with special challenges in communication. During a face-to-face meeting, a participant can pick up valuable information by observing the nonspoken behavior of the other people attending the meeting. An acerbic comment by one person may cause another to flinch. Some attendees may doze off during boring meetings. A clever statement may be met with smiles. However, nonverbal cues are lost when we communicate using most of the communication modalities listed above. (The only exception is the case of video-conferencing.) The flinches, nodding heads, or smiles are lost to participants engaging in e-mail correspondence or participating in teleconferences.

Team members of a virtual project team must be sensitive to the limitations and opportunities associated with whatever communication technology they use. They must determine what constitutes good and bad behavior in the context of specific communication technologies. Inundating team members with trivial, time-wasting e-mail messages is viewed as bad behavior today, when it is common for people to receive 30 to 60 messages in a day. Dominating the conversation during a teleconference is generally considered bad behavior. In contrast, making focused statements (thereby enabling other participants to have a chance to express their views) is considered good behavior.

As time goes on and people become more experienced in employing the new communication technologies, rules are emerging to help define how the technologies should be used to optimize communication. This was evident when the transmission of fax messages began in the mid-1980s. No sooner was the technology introduced than people recognized that fax messages should begin with a cover page that noted to whom the message was sent, from whom it originated, and the number of pages contained in the message. With the advent of teleconferencing, a convention arose that when individuals join the conversation, they should offer their names at the outset of their statement so that all parties to the conversation know who is talking. Similar conventions will arise with all the communication technologies that make virtual projects possible.

VIII.

ESTABLISHING
A PROJECT OFFICE

E STABLISHING A PROJECT OFFICE requires a lot of
effort. As with any worthwhile idea, it demands
great thought and careful planning. It also requires
political sensitivity, because many people in the organization will resist it. The establishment of a project office
should be carried out in two broad phases: selling the
idea of creating a project office, and actually creating it
(see Figure 5).

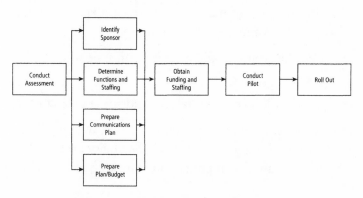

Figure 5.   Implementing a project office

Selling the Idea

Not everyone will embrace the idea that establishing a project office is worthwhile. Some people will complain that it is an unnecessary expense that the organization can ill afford in an era of resource scarcity. Others may view it as yet another layer of bureaucracy that will slow down the organization's conduct of business. Still others will see it as an attempt to take power away from them and put it into the hands of a centralized group.

People who want to establish a project office should realize that they are likely to encounter substantial skepticism and resistance to their efforts. It is important at the outset that project office planners take well-defined steps to educate their colleagues about the need for a project office, and that they describe clearly how it will function. If they want to have support within the organization, they must sell the idea of such an office.

A good starting point is to identify what questions colleagues will raise about the project office. Having good answers to these questions before they surface will help allay the concerns of many of the skeptics. Following is a list of three commonly asked questions:

- Of what value would a project office be to our projects?

- What will it cost to establish and run a project office?

- To what extent will the project office, with its focus on establishing standards, kill flexibility and creativity in the activities of project staff working in the field?

The Value of a Project Office

Project offices provide value both to project team members and customers. For project team members, a fully functioning project office can be an invaluable source of support. Project offices can supply team members with mentors, consultants, and just-in-time training. They offer guidance on project management standards and can provide team members with the tools they need to do their jobs effectively. In addition, they can maintain a library of past project management solutions that might be reusable on new projects.

Experience shows that customers are strong supporters of the concept of project offices. They see the establishment of a project office as a visible sign of an organization's commitment to pursue project management in the best way possible. The existence of a project office increases their confidence that the project team with which they work has the support it needs to operate as competently as possible.

Maintenance Costs

Some skeptics are nervous that a project office will add to the costs of doing business without generating corresponding savings. Establishing and running a project office will not be cheap, particularly if the office aspires to be a full-service provider.

Project management today is in a similar position to that of the quality movement in the 1970s and 1980s. At that time, naysayers questioned the cost effectiveness of establishing quality management programs. They maintained that the cost of quality programs would not offset any savings they might realize. However, experience showed that well-conceived quality programs paid for themselves quickly. The real question turned out to be: Can an organization afford not to establish solid quality management programs?

Recent studies suggest that only a minority of projects achieve their objectives on time, within budget, and according to specifications. (See, for example, studies carried out by the Standish Group and the Gartner Group.) The old *ad hoc* approaches to implementing projects have not produced commendable results. If the experience of the quality management movement is a meaningful guide, it would appear that a comprehensive approach to project management—a major feature of project offices—will pay for itself quickly.

The costs of establishing and running a project office may be less shocking than the figures would suggest, because in most organizations the costs of doing project work are spread throughout the organization and are probably substantial, although not actually known. The cost of maintaining a project office could be less than or equal to the cumulative cost of conducting project efforts without such an office. To the extent that a project office can create an environment in which teams do the job right the first time, project costs will drop dramatically.

Creativity, Flexibility, and the Project Office

As organizations grow, they often debate the relative merits of conducting centralized versus decentralized operations. Each approach has its strengths and weaknesses. Centralized operations tend to produce higher levels of consistency and enable control to be exercised more directly. Although they may generate solutions that are out of touch with events in the field, and they tend to sustain slow decision-making processes. In contrast, decentralized operations tend to generate solutions that reflect real conditions in the field, and they empower workers to make decisions speedily. However, consistency may be lost and control is weak.

Project offices reflect a bias toward centralized decision making, but this does not necessarily mean a loss of creativity and flexibility in decision making in the field. A well-configured project office is set up to support team members to do their jobs more effectively, not to tell them *how* to do their jobs. Project workers in the field are encouraged to operate as creatively and independently as they can, but their independence will be constrained according to procedures defined by the project office.

The champions of the project office must make clear to their colleagues that they will serve the community. Their job is not to bully people, but to support them by maintaining an orderly environment.

Establishing a Communication Plan

At the outset of their efforts, the project office champions should establish a communication plan to implement conscious communication activities about the project office. A typical communication plan has several components to it. For example, a single spokesperson should be identified to speak on behalf of the project office. Mechanisms for collecting feedback from colleagues should be established (for example, by walking around and talking to them). Means for regularly educating colleagues on the office's activities should be developed (for example, by issuing a newsletter).

Implementing a Project Office

Once the creation of the project office has been authorized, attention focuses on start-up issues, which must be resolved before the office can open. Questions include:

- What functions should the project office carry out?
- How will the office be staffed?
- Where will the office be situated, both organizationally and physically?

Proper Project Office Functions

As noted in Chapter II, project offices can carry out a wide range of activities. On a modest level, they may do only one or two things, such as develop project management standards and maintain scheduling software. On a more grandiose plane, they can be full-service providers, offering services in consulting, mentoring, training, maintaining standards, maintaining scheduling software, and serving as the organization's home to project managers.

One of the first issues that must be resolved when establishing a project office is to define what it should do.

Staffing

Staffing of the project office is sensitive to two issues. First, is the project office to play the central role in guiding project management in the organization? Second, what range of functions will the project office support?

If the project office has been established to serve in a simple support and facilitation role, then staffing becomes an elementary matter—the office will contain only a few people. It might have a director who has years of experience in managing projects, one or two professional associates who have solid project management skills, and a clerical specialist who can handle basic office chores—word processing, filing, and basic communication with the rest of the organization. Or, the "office" might consist of one jack-of-all-trades who serves as the organization's principal project management guru. The chief function of this simple configuration is to operate in an *ad hoc* fashion to address project management issues as they arise within the organization.

If the project office is designed to play a central role in guiding an organization's project efforts, staffing grows more complex. The office will be run by a director who is supported by more professional associates and administrative personnel. The director should be granted a substantial amount of formal authority to demonstrate the seriousness with which upper management views the effective management of projects. The director's position within the organization chart should be equivalent to the position of high-level functional managers.

The professional associates will reflect a wide range of experience and skills, from novices (who can proffer technical assistance on basic budgeting, scheduling, resource allocation, and computer software issues) to experts (who are able to address just about any project-related issue). Administrative personnel should have basic skills in such areas as word processing, database maintenance, and office communications.

Staffing of the project office is also sensitive to the kinds of efforts the office will carry out. If the office develops project management standards and procedures for the organization, then highly experienced professional staff must exist to serve these functions. If the office serves a consulting, mentoring, and training function, then seasoned project professionals must be available.

Location

The project office should be situated wherever it makes sense. In many financial institutions, such as banks and real estate companies, project offices are established in the information systems departments. This makes sense, because many of the projects conducted by financial organizations require linking people and organizations electronically, and the heart of that effort usually lies in the information services department. In engineering-based organizations, the project office might be linked to the organization's industrial engineering activities. In yet other situations, the project office might be treated as an independent functional operation along the lines of contracting, sales, and finance departments.

Encouraging Project Management Certification

As noted in Chapter VI, PMI has initiated a certification program to test the basic competencies of project professionals in nine areas: scope management, time management, cost management, human resource management, risk management, quality management, procurement management, communication management, and integration management. People who pass the certification process are designated certified project management professionals (PMPs).

This certification process attempts to assess the knowledge-based competencies of project professionals. Certification provides *prima facie* evidence that an individual possesses current knowledge about best practices in project management. Some well-known organizations that encourage or require their project workers to become certified include: AT&T, Lucent Technologies, NCR, ABB, Bell Atlantic, Bell South, IBM, Motorola, Hewlett-Packard, Nynex, US West, the Defense Systems Management College, and the Army Corps of Engineers.

FURTHER READING

Frame, J. D. *Managing Projects in Organizations: How to Make the Best Use of Time, Techniques, and People* (revised edition). San Francisco: Jossey-Bass, 1995.

Frame, J. D. *The New Project Management: Tools for an Age of Rapid Change, Corporate Reengineering, and Other Business Realities.* San Francisco: Jossey-Bass, 1994.

Peters, T. J. *Liberation Management.* New York: Knopf, 1992.

Project Management Institute Standards Committee. *A Guide to the Project Management Body of Knowledge.* Upper Darby, Pennsylvania: Project Management Institute, 1996.

Wideman, R. M. *A Framework for Project and Program Management Integration.* Upper Darby, Pennsylvania: Project Management Institute, 1991.

ABOUT THE AUTHORS

Thomas R. Block is a project management consultant
and lecturer specializing in establishing project offices,
project start-ups, project intervention and recovery,
and just-in-time training. While at Electronic Data
Systems, he directed the Project Management Consulting
Group (eastern region). He has presented papers on
project management at the Project Management Institute
(PMI) seminar/symposia, Project World, and Project
Leadership conferences. He is a certified project man-
agement professional and has an MBA from Syracuse
University and a bachelor of business administration in
accounting from Canisius College in Buffalo, New York.
He is also a visiting corporate fellow at the George
Washington University International Center for Project
Management Excellence.

J. Davidson Frame is director of the International Center
for Project Management Excellence at George Washington
University. From 1990 through 1996 he was also director
of certification at the Project Management Institute. Begin-
ning in December 1996 he became director of educational
services at PMI. He has published more than 40 scholarly
articles and four books.